Learning LOL

Welcome to my class on Creative Writing! My name is Professor Charlie, and I am so excited to show you all the fun things my assistant and I have been learning. My assistant is my mom, and she is super helpful! She reads all of the research we do together out loud, takes me for walks when it is time for a break, finds yummy treats for the both of us to share, and also does all the typing since she has fingers and thumbs, and I only have paws, and the most important thing of all, she gives the best belly rubs. My job is to give her fun ideas to look up, to keep her warm with cuddles, and to try not to bark at the mailman. I make no promises about the last one. We make a really great team!

Every Friday, if the weather is nice, my assistant and I love to have a picnic in our backyard for lunch. I love sitting outside with the wind in my ears and eating some yummy food that I helped pick out. Today, we had some yummy chicken that my assistant's husband made, pretzels, carrots, a peanut butter cookie for my assistant, a gravy dog bone for me, and our favorite snack, peanut butter and apples. After finishing our food, we laid down on our blanket with our bellies full and stared up at the sky. As we lay there and staring at the clouds, we started seeing shapes in the clouds. I thought one of the clouds looked like a dinosaur with a long neck but had a fish body and webbed feet like a duck. My mom, sorry, I meant my assistant, said she saw a rocking horse racing a dolphin. We both started to laugh. We lay there for the next 20 minutes and talked about all the funny things we saw in the clouds. By the time we were done my cheeks hurt because I was laughing so much! We decided we were all done with our picnic and needed to return to our office and get back to work.

After cleaning up from our picnic, we returned to our office and started talking about what our next book could be. My assistant sat down on our cozy sofa, and I very slowly, like a ninja, got up on the sofa and laid down on her lap. I don't think she noticed! We sat silently for a little while, trying to think of something our pup pals would like to do or would like to learn. I do my best thinking when I am lying on my back and getting belly rubs, and thankfully, my assistant is amazing at this! She is the best! As I lay there, all I could think about was all of the silly clouds we saw during our lunch and how funny they were. I asked my assistant if she could make up a silly story about a rocking horse and a dolphin racing. She gave a big smile, said, of course,

thought for a minute, and began her story. Her story was about a rocking horse and a dolphin racing to see who would be the first to find the magical silver saddle. It was lost on an island somewhere in the Pacific Ocean, and whoever found it could wear it and be able to fly in the sky, walk on the land, and swim deep under the water. Her story was so funny. My favorite part of the story was when the dolphin found the saddle and grew frog legs to walk on land!

When she was done telling her story, she asked me if I could make a new kind of animal using different animal body parts. This was going to be super fun! I jumped up, ran to the desk, and grabbed a piece of paper and a pencil. I drew a giraffe's body and neck with eight octopus tentacles, a chicken head, a lemur tail, and big bird wings. I tried my best to draw my new animal, but it is a little tricky when you have paws and not hands. My assistant told me that I did a fabulous job, and she taped it to the side of the filing cabinet. As I sat there looking at my silly drawing, I realized I had an idea for a new book! A creative writing book!

My assistant and I love making funny puns, sentences, and stories, so I told her my idea, and she loved it! We sat all day thinking of all the funny things we could write about, and we came up with so many. After we were done thinking about funny things to write about, I started to think about what other kinds of things my pup pals would like to write about. We thought for a while about what else was fun, and my assistant thought of something great: holidays! I love all of the holidays! After doing research on different holidays, we thought of different questions my pup pals could answer about them. Did you know that there are more than 20 holidays around the world? I had no idea but was excited to learn about these new holidays. My favorite part of the holiday is the food. My assistant said during these new holidays, we will try the different foods that go with each one. I told her I hoped there would be green eggs and ham that we could eat!! It is my favorite thing to eat and one of my favorite books, especially when I was a young pup! She knew this was one of my favorites and told me on March 2nd, we could make it because it was Dr. Seuss Day. Who knew this man was a great children's writer, chef, and had his own holiday? She told me he said something amazing, "Why fit in when you were born to stand out?" I thought about this for a few minutes and then began to smile. I agreed with what Dr. Seuss said. I love beginning who I am. I think I am the only dog who loves to learn new things and then teach them to my amazing pup pals. I would not change anything

about myself. I am PAW-tastic! I asked her if anyone else said anything smart and helpful, and she said yes! So, we spent some time looking up important people and the smart things they said and wrote them all down for you.

We hope that you enjoy our book about creative writing. Please don't worry if you don't understand something or don't know who someone is. I made sure everything was super easy to look up if you didn't understand. Looking up things you don't know is a wonderful way for you to learn how to be a researcher like me! But please ask an adult if it is ok to use the computer before you begin your research. Manners and safety first! I hope you enjoy our book, our new pup pal. We will see you for your next lesson!

Tara & Charlie Morrish

Professor Charlie

Smokey

*Photos by
Scarlet Morrish*

Charlie's Drawing

Learning LOL

Where learning language online is fun!

We want to thank you, from the bottom of our paws to the tips of our ears, for buying our book! We hope you enjoyed reading it as much as we enjoyed writing and researching it. We are also excited to share that you can join us on our website soon. Here, you can view your favorite topics with videos, maps, pictures, interactive worksheets, and flashcards. To make entering the classroom easier, scan the QR code, but remember to ask your grown-up before going online. See you there!

Have fun learning online!

Have fun learning with more books!

Where learning language online is fun!

Table of Contents

Where learning language online is fun!

Where learning language online is fun!

Learning LOL

Where learning language online is fun!

Fun Ideas

Where learning language online is fun!

Learning LOL

Where learning language online is fun!

Fun Writing Ideas

1) Write a short story about an animal going to space. What kind of animal is it? How will they get to outer space? Why are they going to outer space? What kind of things do they encounter?

2) What if a snowman came to life? What would you do? Where did you find the snowmen, or did you make them? Can you offer them some clothes? How would you keep the snowman from melting if it got too warm outside?

3) Write a story about an animal going on an underwater adventure. What kind of animal would go? How are they able to get around underwater? Why are they going, and what are they looking for? What types of things do they see underwater? Make sure you describe everything in great detail.

4) What if you could host a fancy party? What kind of party would you have? What type of venue would you have for your party? What would people have to wear? What kind of foods would you have? What will people do? Will people be dancing, live entertainment, and bungee jumping, or will they just stand around and talk?

5) Invent a new kind of candy. What kind of ingredients will it be made out of? How would you market your candy? Do you have a logo or catchphrase? How much will you sell it for? What does the packaging look like? Does this candy do anything special? Who would buy your candy?

6) If you could have a trained wild animal for a pet, what kind of animal would you have and why? Where would you keep this animal, and where would they sleep? How would you afford to feed it? What kinds of things would you do together?

Fun Writing Ideas

7) What if you could trade places with animals for one day? What animal would you want to be? Why would you choose this animal? What kinds of things would you do for the day? Do you think you would enjoy eating the same as your animal or being in the same habitat?

8) If you could compete in the Olympics, which sport or sports would you choose? How would you prepare yourself for such a competitive competition? What would you do to prepare to go to another country? What would you do while you were there during your downtime?

9) Imagine that you could become a magical creature at the snap of your fingers. What kind of creature would you be? How do you change back into a person? Do you have magical powers, or can you do something cool without magic? What kinds of things would you do after you changed? Would you help people, or would you play tricks?

10) Create a dinosaur. Would it be a carnivore, a herbivore, or an omnivore? What would it look like? Would it have scales, feathers, fins, arms, wings, plates, a tail, a big head, and a small body (Be creative)? Where would it live, and who does it live with? What are some of their characteristics? Did they survive the meteor that killed the other dinosaurs?

11) What if someone gave you a private island and 100 million dollars? What would you do with the island? Where would you want your island to be in the world, somewhere cold or somewhere tropical? What would you name it? What would you build there? Would you make a home on the island or use it for a vacation getaway or business?

Where learning language online is fun!

Fun Writing Ideas

12) What is your favorite time of year? What kinds of things do you like to do during this time? Is there a special event or holiday? What is something you dislike?

13) Create a new animal using the body parts of different kinds of animals. Where would this animal live, and what would it eat? Would it be kind and gentle or aggressive and feared? Would it be a pet or a wild animal?

14) What is the grossest thing you have ever eaten? Did you want to try it, or did someone tell you it was good and they were lying? Where were you when you tried it? Was the food gross-looking and ended up tasting good? Did it look delicious and taste horrible, or gross looking and tasting?

15) What have you always wanted but were too scared to try? Why are you afraid to do it? Is there anything or anyone that could change your mind about trying it?

16) Which would you choose if you could live in the mountains, the sky, the desert, or underwater? What kind of house would you have (be creative and descriptive)? How would you get there? Would you build a city or home for yourself, friends, and family? How would you get food?

17) Invent a new kind of clothing with special powers. What are your unique abilities, and how would you use them? What materials would it be made of, and what would it look like? Could you wear it all year long or only at certain times? Do you have only one, or can anyone buy it? If anyone can believe it, how much will it cost?

Where learning language online is fun!

Fun Writing Ideas

18) If you could spend the day with any historical person, who would it be, and why? Where would you take them, and what would you do? What kind of questions would you ask them?

19) Invent something new that would help Mom and Dad. Will it help them at home or work? How would your parents benefit from it? How does it work?

20) What is your favorite plant or tree? Where does it grow? When does it bloom? Is it a carnivore? How do you take care of it? Have you seen it in person or only in a book, on TV, or online?

21) Invent your club. Will it be for school, the community, the church, or something completely different? Who can join your club? What does your club do? Do you have to pass some kind of test before you can become a member? When and where do you meet?

22) You are having a picnic, and the king and queen are coming! Will it be super fancy, or will you show them how ordinary people have a picnic? Where will you have your picnic? What kind of food and drinks will you serve? What kind of activities will you do? What if it rains? Do you have a backup plan?

23) What if one day you became ruler of the whole world? What kind of ruler would you be? Would you be kind and try to help everyone, or would you be cruel and enslave the world? Where would your capital be? What would people help advise you, or will you do everything by yourself? What kind of laws would you have, and what happens if someone breaks them?

24) What would it look like if you could build a playground for animals? Would it be for one kind or many kinds of animals? Where would you create it? What kind of materials would you use? Who would take care of the animals and playground?

Fun Writing Ideas

25) If a UFO landed on Earth, what do you think would happen? What would the aliens look like (be descriptive)? Are they friendly and willing to help us? Are they aggressive and want to enslave the people of Earth? What does their ship look like? How would the people of Earth react to seeing a UFO and aliens?

26) Invent a new kind of vehicle. What type of materials would you use to build it? Are there unique features on the inside or the outside of the car? What color will you paint it? Will you drive it, or will it drive itself? How many people will fit inside? What kind of speeds will it reach?

27) If you could live in a different year, what year would it be? Why did you choose this time, and do you hope to achieve anything there? How would you make a living? Are you able to return to your current year?

28) Design a restaurant. Where would it be located? How will you decorate the inside and outside of the restaurant? What food is on the menu? Do you have a serving staff, or is it only take-out food? If so, are they real people, or is the food served differently? Will your food be expensive or cheap?

29) If you could change into any bug, which would you choose? Why did you choose this bug? What kind of environment would you enjoy? How long would you want to stay a bug? What would be some of the dangers of being that bug?

30) What if the dinosaurs never became extinct? How would the world be different? Would humans be able to live how we do now in buildings, or would we have to hide in the mountains like our ancestors? Are the dinosaurs wild, feared, or trained to be our pets or help us daily? How would we share Earth's resources with such big, dangerous/friendly animals?

Fun Writing Ideas

31) One day, you are walking on the beach, and you find a bottle. After rubbing the lamp, a Genie appears and grants you three wishes. There are special rules with these wishes. You must wish for something good for someone else. Who would you make a wish for, and what would it be?

32) What is the most important item you own? Why is it so important to you, and who or how did you get it? Where do you keep it? Do you do anything special with this item? What would you do if you lost it?

33) If you could be famous, how would you want to achieve this? Would you like to invent something, be an actor, be an athlete, be someone in the government, or be an explorer? Why? How would you use your fame?

34) Teaching is a challenging job. Imagine you had to teach a week of classes. Which subject would it be? How would you prepare for your classes? Would you have any teaching assistants?

35) You visit your grandparent's house and find a locked trap door under a tree in the backyard. What do you do? Do you go and tell someone, or do you try and open it yourself? If you can open it, what do you find inside?

36) Describe your dream birthday party. Where would you have the party? Is there a theme or a color scheme? Who will you invite? Will there be activities for people to do at the party? What kind of cake or dessert will you have? Will you serve food and snacks? If so, what kind?

Fun Writing Ideas

37) What field of study would be if you could be a scientist? Why would you choose this field, and what do you hope to accomplish? Would you want to be famous or work behind the scenes?

38) You and a friend are walking on the beach, and you find a chest washed up on shore. What does it look like? What do you and your friend do with it? If you open the chest, what do you find inside, and what will you do with it? Is anyone going to be looking for it? If so, who will be looking?

39) What kind of farm would you have if you could have your farm? Would your farm be big and commercial or small and personal? Would you grow fruits and vegetables or raise livestock? What kind of help would you need to keep the farm running?

40) What games do you like playing with friends and family? Are you or the people you play with very competitive? Do you want to play more physical games or sit down for more relaxing games? What is your favorite game, and who taught you how to play it?

Learning LOL

Where learning language online is fun!

Holidays

Where learning language online is fun!

Holidays Writing Topics

New Year's Eve & New Year's Day

★ What is New Year's Eve, and why do we celebrate it?

★ How do you celebrate New Year's Day?

★ What was your New Year's resolution this year? Did you have one last year? If so, were you able to keep it?

★ Why do people make New Year's resolutions? What is the funniest one you have ever heard?

★ What was the best year of your life that you could remember?

★ What was the best and worst part of last year? Name one success and one failure you had last year.

★ How will this year be different from last year? What kind of goals do you have planned to accomplish? Will you focus more on work, school, sports, personal relationships, being more social, working on yourself, or something else?

★ What is the best memory you made last year? How did this moment make you feel? What memories do you hope to make this year? Who do you expect is in these memories?

★ If you could go to another country for a New Year's Eve celebration, which country would it be? Why? Who would you bring?

★ People say that with the new year, you have a fresh start; this is the best time to make positive changes. Do you agree or disagree with this?

★ What is something new you will try this year? Is it something that you just learned about and are excited to try, or is it something that you are afraid of and want to overcome?

Holidays Writing Topics

New Year's Eve & New Year's Day

★ Are any significant events happening this year with you or your family? How do you feel about it?

★ What do you do to celebrate this holiday? Do you see friends and family or have a quiet night at home?

★ Do you watch the ball drop on the TV, or have you ever been there in person?

★ What is the first country to start the New Year, and which is the last?

★ Do all countries celebrate New Year's Eve?

★ If you could have your ball drop, what would you drop? What state or country would you pick?

★ What year would you choose if you could travel back to any year?

★ Do some states or cities have their ball drop? If so, what do they drop?

Martin Luther King Jr. Day

★ Why is Martin Luther King Jr. important? How did he impact the lives of thousands?

★ Would you have the courage to lead and stand up for the injustices you see?

★ How did segregation affect people's lives? Is it still happening today?

★ What is racism? How does this affect people's lives?

Holidays Writing Topics

<u>Martin Luther King Jr. Day</u>

★ How can you make your community a better place to live or bring positive change to others?

★ If you could ask Martin Luther King Jr. one question, what would it be?

★ Why is Martin Luther King Jr. Day a national holiday?

★ When did you first hear the speech "I Have a Dream," and how did it make you feel after you heard it?

<u>Groundhog Day</u>

★ What is Groundhog Day? Why is it a groundhog that predicts the weather?

★ If I could predict the weather, I would predict..?

★ What would you do if one day your shadow came to life? Would you be scared, or would it be the coolest thing ever?

★ Do other countries have events like Groundhog Day that will predict something for the future?

★ What would happen if we had winter forever? How would your life change? Are there any advantages or disadvantages to having only one season?

★ What is your favorite season? What kinds of things do you like to do?

★ What is your favorite thing to do in the Winter?

★ What is your favorite thing to do in Spring?

Where learning language online is fun!

Holidays Writing Topics

Lunar New Year or Spring Festival

★ Why do we celebrate Chinese New Year? In what countries is the holiday celebrated?

★ What is the meaning of the red envelope? Will you receive one? If so, from whom?

★ What is your Chinese Zodiac? Do you think you have the same characteristics?

★ How does your family celebrate the Lunar New Year? Do you gather with friends and family and have a big party? Do you and your family go on a vacation during the holiday?

★ What foods will you have on Chinese New Year? Who will do most of the cooking, or does the whole family help?

★ What is this year's Chinese Zodiac animal? What does this mean, and what are the different characteristics of this animal?

★ What is your best Spring Festival memory?

★ At the end of the Spring Festival, which holiday starts the next day? Why is it celebrated?

★ Why is the color red so crucial during this holiday?

Valentine's Day

★ Who is the most special person in your life? What makes them unique to you?

★ Who are the people in your life that you love?

★ Talk about a time that you felt loved and appreciated.

Holidays Writing Topics

Valentine's Day

★ How do you celebrate Valentine's Day? Do you go to the store and spend money or make something yourself?

★ Where did the holiday come from, and why do we celebrate it?

★ What animal do you love the most, and do they love you back? How can you tell?

★ What is the best thing you ever received on Valentine's Day, and who was your Valentine?

Presidents Day

★ Who was the first president of the United States? Did he want to be president at first?

★ Which president had the shortest term? Why was it so quick?

★ Did any president ever die in office? If so, how or why?

★ Did every president live in the White House? When was it built, and why was this location chosen?

★ How many presidents have we had? Who had the most impact on the country?

★ Who is the president now? Are they doing a good job? If not, what would you say to the president?

★ What things would you do if you were President?

★ Do you think being President is hard? Why or why not?

Learning LOL

Where learning language online is fun!

Holidays Writing Topics

Presidents Day

★ Do all countries have a president or another form of government? Is one form better than another?

★ If you could meet with any president, past or current, and spend the day together, where would you go, and what kind of conversations would you have?

Daylight Savings Time

★ What is Daylight Savings Time? Why did it start?

★ Do we still need to have Daylight Saving Time? Why or why not?

★ What are some of the negative things associated with Daylight Saving Time?

★ Does every state in the U.S.A. observe the time change?

★ Does every country observe Daylight Saving Time?

St. Patrick's Day

★ Do you celebrate St. Patrick's Day? If so, how?

★ Was St. Patrick a living person? If so, what did he accomplish?

★ What animal did St. Patrick supposedly drive out of Ireland?

★ Why do we celebrate St. Patrick's Day in America? What country did the holiday originate from?

★ What kinds of food are popular on St. Patrick's Day? Have you ever tried any of them?

Holidays Writing Topics

St. Patrick's Day

★ What would you do if you caught a Leprechaun?

★ What treasure would you hope to find at the rainbow's end? Do you wish it was a chest of gold or the leprechaun?

★ What kind of "Good Luck" would you have if you found a 4-leaf clover? Where did this myth start, and why?

★ How can you create good luck, or do you think the universe makes your luck for you?

Passover

★ What is Passover? Why is it important?

★ How do you and your family celebrate Passover? Do you go to church or do something else that is special to your family?

★ How do you think you would have felt leaving Egypt? Would you be scared or excited to leave all you have ever known, even if it was terrible, for the unknown across the desert?

★ Would you have left Egypt if you knew you would be in the desert for 40 years and face many hardships?

★ What was the biggest challenge the Jews overcame? Are they still overcoming anything?

★ What was the best thing to happen to the Jews during their 40 years in the desert?

★ What was the most significant thing you had to overcome? Did you overcome it by yourself, or did you have help?

Holidays Writing Topics

Easter

★ Why do we celebrate Easter? Does every country celebrate this holiday?

★ Why are "bunnies" and "eggs" associated with Easter? And where did this begin?

★ How do you and your family celebrate Easter? Do you go to church, have a big dinner, or go on vacation?

★ Is Easter always on the same day every year? Why?

★ What would you do if you woke up and were the Easter Bunny? What extraordinary things would you do?

★ What is your favorite and least favorite Easter candy?

★ How did people live during the time that Jesus lived? Did they have easy or hard lives?

★ What do you think Jesus thinks to himself as he watches over us today? Would he be proud or disappointed?

★ Why do people give up something for Lent? Did you give up anything for Lent? If so, what and why?

★ How would you react if Jesus suddenly appeared before you? How would this make you feel, and what would you say?

★ There have been many different versions of what Jesus looked like. Describe how you think he looks and what he would wear. Remember what year it was and what part of the world he lived in.

★ What would happen to the Christian religion if Jesus's resurrection had never happened?

Holidays Writing Topics
Ramadan

★ How do you and your family celebrate Ramadan?

★ Why is Ramadan important, and why is it celebrated?

★ What is your favorite thing to eat for Suhoor, and who cooks it? What time do you get up in the morning to eat?

★ What is the first thing you eat for iftar after the sun goes down? Do you have any traditional foods every year?

★ Do you think prayer is essential in a person's life? Why or why not?

★ Does your family decorate and invite friends and family over for Iftar? Or do you go over to someone else's house?

★ Why is Fasting important for Ramadan? Are there certain things a person must Fast from during this holiday? Describe the most challenging part about Fasting.

★ Does your family give to charity during Ramadan? If so, which ones and why is it essential to your family?

Eid al-Fitr

★ What is Eid al-Fitr, and when does it occur?

★ How many days does Eid al-Fitr last?

★ Does your family give to charity during Eid al-Fitr? If so, which ones and why is it essential to your family?

★ Does your family have any unique traditions during Eid al-Fitr? If so, what are they?

Learning LOL

Where learning language online is fun!

Holidays Writing Topics

Cinco de Mayo

★ What battle in Mexico does this holiday commemorate? Was it a big or small battle?

★ How do you and your family celebrate Cinco de Mayo? What is your favorite and least favorite part of the day?

★ How would you plan your perfect Cinco de Mayo party? What kind of food, decorations, and games would you play?

★ How have Mexican and American cultures influenced each other over the years? Is it a good thing or a bad thing? What other things do you think they could learn from each other?

★ Why do you think Cinco de Mayo is so famous in America?

★ What is your favorite part of Mexican culture? Is it essential to learn about other cultures?

Mother's Day

★ How do you celebrate your mom on Mother's Day?

★ What is the most thoughtful thing your mother has done for you?

★ What is the most thoughtful thing you have done for your mother?

★ What makes your mother so unique?

★ How could you make your mother's life easier?

★ When I am sad or hurt, my mom does...?

★ The best memory I have of my mom is...?

★ The thing that makes my mom the happiest is...?

Where learning language online is fun!

Holidays Writing Topics

Mother's Day

★ Do you consider any of your friend's moms like your own mom? If so, why?

★ Where would you go if you could take your mom anywhere? Why did you pick this place?

★ Has your mom ever coached a sports team or led a club you were a part of? If so, how did you feel about your mom coaching your team or leading your club?

★ If your mom was a superhero, what would her name be, and what would her superpowers be?

★ Can you have more than one mom? Do you have a stepmom? If so, what kinds of things do you like to do together? Do you have any new brothers or sisters?

Memorial Day

★ Why do we celebrate Memorial Day? Why is it the last Monday of May?

★ How do you and your family celebrate Memorial Day?

★ Have you ever lost someone close to you? How did you feel after you lost them? What do you do to remember them?

★ Write a short story or a paragraph about a veteran returning from war. It can be fiction or nonfiction.

★ Does your family have a barbeque for Memorial Day? If so, what kinds of food do you have, and what is your favorite? Who is in charge of the grill?

Holidays Writing Topics

Memorial Day

★ Why do most people barbecue for this holiday?

★ Why must we remember the men and women who have served and died for our country?

★ What is a War Memorial? Can you think of any in America?

★ Have you ever been to or been in a Memorial Day Parade? Why do we have parades around the country to celebrate?

★ Do you agree or disagree with American troops helping other countries?

Juneteenth

★ What is Juneteenth, and when do we celebrate it?

★ Why was the importance of the Emancipation Proclamation so significant?

★ Who are some of the important historical figures in African American history?

★ What was the importance of the underground railroad? Who are some of the historical figures who are associated with it?

★ What was the last state to end slavery? Why did it take so long to free the enslaved people in this state?

Holidays Writing Topics

Father's Day

★ What are the best things about your dad?

★ Write a short story about the funniest thing you can remember your dad doing.

★ Does your dad tell bad "dad jokes"? If so, what is the worst one?

★ Has your dad ever coached a sports team or led a club you were in? If so, how did you feel about your dad coaching your team or leading your club?

★ If your dad was a superhero, what would his name be, and what would his superpowers be?

★ Can you have more than one dad? Do you have a stepdad? If so, what kinds of things do you like to do together? Do you have any new brothers or sisters?

★ What is the kindest thing you have ever done for your dad?

★ What is your best memory of your dad?

Independence Day or The 4th of July

★ Why do we celebrate Independence Day, and why is it important?

★ When was the Constitution signed? Who were some of the famous men who signed it?

★ Were any women or people of color involved with the Constitution's writing or signing?

★ How would America look today if they didn't win the Revolutionary War and gained freedom from England?

Learning LOL

Where learning language online is fun!

Holidays Writing Topics

Independence Day or The 4th of July

★ Our Founding Fathers wrote the Constitution over 230 years ago. Would you change any part of it? If so, which parts and why?

★ How do you stay safe when lighting fireworks and sparklers?

★ Do you think that every 50 years or so, the Constitution should be rewritten to fit the changing American life and to keep up with modern times?

★ Why did people leave Europe to come to the New World? Would you have been brave enough to make the trip?

★ Where did the first people settle, and what were their living conditions?

★ Did the first settlers encounter other people when they reached the New World?

★ What should you bring to a new land by boat to prepare your new home? Should you rely on the resources you might find when you reach land?

★ How does your family celebrate the 4th of July? Do you have a BBQ and light off fireworks?

★ What foods do you like to eat on the 4th of July? Are certain people in charge of bringing certain foods to your celebration?

★ What does our flag represent? Who designed the first flag, and when?

★ Do you travel anywhere for a holiday? If so, where do you go and who do you take with you?

★ What are your favorite kinds of fireworks? Do you like to light sparklers?

Holidays Writing Topics

Labor Day

★ When is Labor Day, and how do you celebrate it?

★ How does having a solid workforce help your country's economy?

★ Have you ever had a job? If so, what was it, and what were the pros and cons?

★ What would happen if everyone stopped working and went on vacation? What would happen?

★ How does your family celebrate Labor Day? Do you have a BBQ with family and friends or a relaxing day before school the next day?

★ Since Labor Day is the unofficial end of summer, what was the best part of your summer?

★ Why should we celebrate "working people"?

★ Who are some people in your community who help keep you safe?

★ At what age do you think people should start and stop working?

★ What do you want to be when you grow up? What steps will you take to achieve this goal?

★ What benefits do all Americans who work receive or should receive?

★ Should there be a day off school the day after a holiday? If so, why?

★ Your town has a massive factory that employs 75% of the town's population. What would happen to the city if the factory shut down?

★ Why is it essential to have a healthy work/life balance? What would happen if you didn't?

Holidays Writing Topics

Indigenous People's Day

★ What is Indigenous People's Day, and why do we celebrate it?

★ Do you know what indigenous tribe lived or still lives in your area?

★ What are some past hardships that indigenous people faced? How did the Europeans treat most of them?

★ How did the native people used to live? What kind of houses did they have? How did they get food and clothes?

★ Should we celebrate Columbus Day? Why or why not?

★ What role do indigenous people play in America today?

★ How would America look today if Europeans had never settled here?

Veterans Day

★ What is Veterans Day, and why do we celebrate it?

★ Do you know anyone who has ever served in the military? If so, what branch did they serve?

★ What are some ways you can honor veterans in your community?

★ Do other countries have veterans?

★ Would you like to serve in the military? If so, what branch and what job would you like to do?

★ Should the draft come back? Should it include women?

★ Are there benefits to having a military draft? If so, what are they?

Holidays Writing Topics

Veterans Day

★ Should everyone serve in the military for a certain amount of years, as other countries do?

★ What are the five different branches of the military? Should Space Force be considered the 6th branch? Why would we need to have a military branch that deals with space?

Diwali

★ When do people celebrate Diwali, and why do they celebrate it?

★ What are the different religions that celebrate Diwali? Does each religion celebrate this holiday for the same reasons? If not, what are the differences?

★ How many days does Diwali last, and what do you do each day?

★ What is the importance of a rangoli? What are they made of, and what designs have you done?

★ One of the most important symbols for Diwali is a "Diyas," or clay lamp. Why are they so important, and where do people put them after lightening them?

★ The 5th day of Diwali is called (depending on which religion) "Bhai Dooj," "Bhai Tika," or "Bhai Bijis," which is a special day for brothers and sisters. Why is it necessary, and what do they do on this day? What if the brother has more than one sister, or what if he has no sisters? What will he do?

★ What are the most popular dishes that people prepare for Diwali? What is your favorite, and who makes it?

Where learning language online is fun!

Holidays Writing Topics

Halloween

★ What is Halloween, and how do people celebrate it?

★ Which holiday did Halloween originate from, and how did they celebrate it?

★ When did Samhain change to All Hallow's Eve, and why?

★ One of the most recognizable decorations for Halloween is a jack-o-lantern. Why did people start doing this, and what was the first jack-o-lantern made from?

★ Why is playing tricks on people a part of Halloween? What are some of the best pranks you have played?

★ When did children start wearing costumes on Halloween?

★ What was the best and worst costume you have ever worn? Why did you wear it, or who made you wear it?

★ What are the best and worst things you have gotten in your candy bag?

★ Who do you go trick-or-treating with? Do you always go to the same house or try different neighborhoods each year?

★ Have you ever visited a haunted house or corn maze? If so, what scared you the most?

★ When did children start going treat-or-treating? What is your favorite kind of candy?

★ Who are some of Halloween's most famous monsters and creatures?

Where learning language online is fun!

Holidays Writing Topics

Halloween

★ What is your favorite scary movie? Why do you like it?

★ Have you ever been to or had a Halloween party? What did they (you) serve, who invited, did you play games, what kind of decorations were there, and who had the best costume?

★ Has someone's costume ever really scared you? If so, what was it?

Thanksgiving

★ When is Thanksgiving, and when do we celebrate it?

★ When did it become an official holiday on the last Thursday of November?

★ How is Thanksgiving different today than in the past?

★ What would have happened if people from Europe had never come to the New World?

★ How did the early Europeans live when they came to the New World?

★ Who was at the first Thanksgiving, and what food did they have?

★ What do you and your family do for Thanksgiving? Do you travel, or do you stay at home?

★ Will you watch the parade on TV or go in person, or are you not really into it?

★ What food does your family serve on your table for this holiday? What is your favorite?

© 2023

Learninglol.com

34

Holidays Writing Topics

<u>Thanksgiving</u>

★ Do you have a favorite dessert? If so, what is it, and how much will you eat?

★ Why do most people eat turkey on this holiday?

★ What are you thankful for this year?

★ Why is it important to show the people in our lives that we are thankful for them?

★ What is something unique that your family does to celebrate this holiday?

★ What is Black Friday? Will you buy anything?

★ Should we start decorating for Christmas before we celebrate Thanksgiving?

<u>Bodhi Day</u>

★ What is Bodhi Day, and why is it celebrated?

★ Why did Siddhartha Gautama give up being a prince of India?

★ What did Siddhartha Gautama do for 49 days, and what happened after the 49 days?

★ What did Siddhartha Gautama change his name to, and why?

★ After he became the Buddha, what did he do?

★ What are the Noble Eightfold Path and the Four Noble Truths? Why are they essential in Buddhism?

Holidays Writing Topics

Bodhi Day

★ Would Siddhartha Gautama not be a wealthy prince of India and just an average person? Would his message mean as much and have the same effect on people?

★ What is "Enlightenment." And how does this affect your daily life?

★ What is a Bodhi tree, and how do you decorate it? Why is it so important?

★ Are there particular foods that people serve on Bodhi Day? If so, what are they?

★ How do you and your family celebrate Bodhi Day? What kind of decorations do you put up in your home?

★ Where is our favorite place to meditate? What helps you get into the right frame of mind?

Hanukkah

★ What is Hanukkah, and why do we celebrate it?

★ Where do you celebrate Hanukkah? Do you go to someone's house, or do they come to yours?

★ Does Hanukkah always start on the same day every year? If not, why?

★ What are some traditional games, foods, decorations, and essential items used during Hanukkah?

★ Do you think everyone should have the right to practice their religion?

Holidays Writing Topics

Hanukkah

★ What is a menorah, what does it represent, and why was it a miracle?

★ What would have happened if the menorah hadn't stayed lit for eight days and ran out of oil?

★ Why do people fry food during this holiday? What are the most popular foods to fry at this time?

Christmas

★ What is Christmas, and when do we celebrate it?

★ What are some of your family's unique traditions on this holiday?

★ Do you like when it snows for Christmas?

★ How do you decorate your house for the holiday?

★ What was the best and worst gift you have ever gotten?

★ Do you travel to see friends and family for Christmas?

★ When you are with your friends and family, do you play any fun games?

★ What is the name of all the reindeer? Who is your favorite?

★ Would you like to be one of Santa's Elves?

★ If you could only buy one gift for someone this year, who would it be for, and what would you buy?

★ Do you have a favorite Christmas movie or book?

Holidays Writing Topics

Christmas

★ What do you think Santa does on his day off? Does he get a day off? What about the elves? Do they have any time off?

★ Who would it be if you met a magic-talking reindeer or a talking snowman?

★ What kinds of cookies does Mrs. Clause make? How many can Santa have?

★ Does your family do anything on Christmas Eve?

★ What would you do if you were a reindeer and saw the others being mean to Rudolph?

★ Do you leave anything out for Santa and his reindeer on Christmas Eve?

★ What is the most incredible Christmas craft you have ever made?

★ If you could decorate the outside of your house, would you have many lights and things on your lawn or nothing?

★ How did the three wise men find Jesus, and what did they bring for him?

★ What do you think would have happened if Jesus was never born?

★ What do you think the city of Bethlehem was like then?

★ Why did the Catholic Church choose December 25th to celebrate Jesus's birth?

Holidays Writing Topics

Christmas

★ If your family does not celebrate, what do you celebrate and when? Do you celebrate Hanika or Kwanza or nothing at all?

Kwanzaa

★ What is Kwanzaa, and why do we celebrate it?

★ Who began Kwanzaa, what country did it start in, and what year did it begin?

★ How many days is Kwanzaa celebrated, and what are the Seven Principals?

★ How do you and your family celebrate Kwanzaa?

★ What are some traditional foods, decorations, and clothing people wear during Kwanzaa?

★ What colors represent Kwanzaa, and what do they stand for?

★ What are the primary symbols of Kwanzaa, and what do they represent?

Where learning language online is fun!

Where learning language online is fun!

Inspirational Quotes

Where learning language online is fun!

Learning LOL

Where learning language online is fun!

Inspirational Quotes

1. **"Why fit in when you were born to stand out?"**

(Dr. Seuss (1904-1991)- American Author "The Lorax" (1971))

How do you "stand out?" Describe the positives and negatives about standing out among peers. Are there any mental challenges with this way of thinking? If so, what are they, and how can you overcome them?

2. **"Do what you can, with what you have, where you are."**

(Theodor Roosevelt (1858-1919)- 26th President of the United States of America (1901-1909))

Can you name a time in your life when you struggled but found the means to help someone else? If so, describe the situation and how you helped.

3. **"Never give up on what you want to do. The person with big dreams is more powerful than one with all the facts."**

(Albert Einstein (1879-1955)- German Theoretical physicist & Mathematician "Theory of Relativity")

What is your biggest dream? How do you hope to accomplish it? Does anyone stand in your way of achieving your goal? How will you convince this person that this is the right choice for your life?

Inspirational Quotes

4. "Don't let what you can't do stop you from doing what you can do."

(John Wooden (1910-2010)- American basketball coach UCLA (1932-1975))

What is something you are not particularly good at but love doing? Why do you keep doing something you may not be very good at? Are there any benefits to this kind of perseverance?

5. "Nothing is particularly hard if you break it down into small jobs."

(Henry Ford (1863-1947)- Founder of Ford Motor Company)

Talk about a time when you had a massive job and thought you could do it yourself but couldn't. When did you realize you needed help, and how did you ask for it?

6. "With great power comes great responsibility."

(Spiderman (1938–)- Superhero)

Was there a time when someone put you in charge of something? What were some of the challenges and rewards you experienced during this time? Did you find it easy or challenging to be in a leadership role, and would you do it again?

Inspirational Quotes

7. **"Be silly, be honest, be kind."**

(Ralph Waldo Emerson (1803-1882)- American Author "Self-Reliance" (1841))

How should you live your life according to this quote? What essential qualities should a person have, and why are they important?

8. **"Success is not how high you have climbed, but how you make a positive difference to the world."**

(Roy T. Bennett (1957-2018)- Zimbabwean politician & Author "The Light in the Heart" (2016)) (Roy T. Bennett Quotes:minimalistquotes.com)

Talk about someone you know who has significantly impacted your life or community. What was the effect, and did you help in any way? How could helping one person help change the world?

9. **"No one is perfect. That's why pencils have erasers."**

(Wolfgang Riebe (?)- British Magician & Author (Magic books)

Discuss a time when you made a mistake. Did your mistake affect only you or others? How did you make things right, and did they forgive you?

Where learning language online is fun!

Inspirational Quotes

10. "If I cannot do great things, I can do small things in a great way."

(Martin Luther King Jr. (1929-1968)- American Leader of the Civil Rights Movement (Famous speech "I Have a Dream" (1963)) & Activist)

What are some ways that everyday people can make a difference in their community? How do you get the people in your neighborhood to care about your city's problems? Can one person make a difference?

11. "Being different isn't a bad thing. It means you're brave enough to be yourself."

(Luna Lovegood (1981−)- Harry Potter (Ravenclaw))

What type of person are you? Are you the type who is strong-minded and will be yourself no matter what others may say about you? Or are you the type who likes to be in the background and follows the crowd not to stand out?

12. "Don't just read the easy stuff. You may be entertained by it, but you will never grow from it."

(Jim Rohn (1930-2009)- American Businessman & Author "7 Strategies for Wealth & Happiness")

What is the most challenging book you have ever read? Why did you read it? Were you able to finish the book? If so, how were you able to complete it? Why is it important to challenge yourself when reading and in life?

Inspirational Quotes

13. **"Just when the caterpillar thought the world was ending, he turned into a butterfly."**

(Chuang Tzu (Around 369 BC-286 BC)- Chinese philosopher & Author "Zhuangzi" (Unknown))

How do you deal with tricky situations? Do you stay calm and think through all of your options? Or do you rush in without thinking and figuring things out as you go? Which way is a better way to deal with challenging situations?

14. **"The more that you read, the more things you will know. The more that you learn, the more places you'll go."**

(Dr. Seuss (1904-1991)- American Author "Green Eggs and Ham" (1960))

What are some of the most influential books you have read? What did they teach you, and can you apply this knowledge to your life? What do you think would have happened if you had never read them?

15. **"We all can dance when we find music we love."**

(Giles Andreae (1966–)- British Author "Rumble in the Jungle" (1996))

What is something that you are passionate about? How do you share this passion with others around you? How would you help someone who was struggling with finding their passion?

Where learning language online is fun!

Inspirational Quotes

16. "It's not what happens to you, but how you react to it that matters."

(Epictetus (55-135)- Greek Stoic philosopher)

Can you remember a time when you overreacted to a situation? What would have happened if you had reacted differently?

17. "When you know better, you do better."

(Maya Angelou (1928-2014)- Author "I Know Why the Caged Bird Sings (1969) & Civil Rights Activist)

Have you ever thought you knew a lot about a topic (religion, politics, racism, education, etc.) and then realized you might have been wrong in your initial thinking after talking to others? How did you deal with this situation?

18. "Make each day your masterpiece."

(John Wooden (1910-2010)- American basketball coach UCLA (1932-1975)

How do you try to make each day a great day? When you have a bad day, how do you deal with it?

Learning LOL

Where learning language online is fun!

Inspirational Quotes

19. "You always pass failure on the way to success."

(Mickey Rooney (1920-2014)- American Actor "Strike Up the Band" (1940))

What is something that you tried to do repeatedly and kept failing? How did this failure make you feel? Did it make you want to work harder or quit? Were you able to persevere and succeed?

20. "Anything is possible. Anything can be."

(Shel Silverstein (1930-1999)- American Author "The Giving Tree" (1964))

What is something that you thought was impossible but were able to accomplish? What steps did you take to achieve these goals? Did you face obstacles?

21. "Children must be taught how to think, not what to think."

(Margaret Mead (1901-1978)- American cultural anthropologist (She studied the people of the Pacific Islands))

How does it make you feel when trying to figure out how to do something yourself, and someone comes up and tells you what to do? How do you deal with this kind of situation?

Learning LOL

Where learning language online is fun!

Inspirational Quotes

22. "When you do the common things in life in an uncommon way, you will command the attention of the world."

(George Washington Carver (1864-1943)- American agricultural scientist (Discovered over 300 uses for peanuts)

Can you name a time when you or someone else thought "outside the box" and achieved something amazing? How did others treat you during this time, and how did it make you feel?

23. "You must be the change you wish to see in the world."

(Mahatma Gandhi (1869-1948)- Indian Activist & Leader of the Indian Nationalist Movement against British rule)

Can one person make a difference in the world? How would they accomplish this change? What would be the best way to get their message out? What if others stand in their way? Should they give up or try even harder?

24. "Only those who dare to fail greatly can ever achieve greatly."

(Robert F. Kennedy (1925-1968)- 64th United States Attorney General (1944-1946) & U.S. Senator)

Talk about a time when you wanted to do something and failed, then gave up. Did you learn anything from this failure? What could you have achieved if you had not given up? How did it make you feel?

Inspirational Quotes

25. "Judge your success by what you had to give up to get it."

(Dalai Lama XIV (1935–) - The 14th highest Tibetan spiritual leader (1950))

Have you ever had to give something up to follow your dreams? What was it, and were there any consequences? Was giving up something worth what you got in return? Would you do it again?

26. "Success is a state of mind. If you want success, start thinking of yourself as a success."

(Joyce Brothers (1927- 2013)- American psychologist, Author of "How to Get Whatever You Want Out of Life," and TV star)

How does one start to think of themselves as successful if they haven't achieved anything yet? What kinds of steps could a person take to start thinking this way? What is the importance of a positive frame of mind?

27. "If you have good thoughts, they will shine out of your face like sunbeams, and you will always look lovely."

(Roald Dahl (1916-1990)- British Author "James and the Giant Peach" (1961))

What is the importance of always having a positive attitude, even in a bad situation? Is it hard to have this kind of attitude even during dark times? What do you think of people who can do this?

Inspirational Quotes

28. "We know what we are but know not what we may be."

(Shakespeare (1564-1616)- English Playwright, Actor & Poet "Romeo and Juliet" (1595-1596))

What kind of life do you want to have in 10 years? Do you think you will be in a corporate job, traveling the world, or famous? What kind of relationships will you have with people? Will you be married with kids or single? Where will you live, and what type of home will you have? Is it important to consider what you want your life to be like later in life or just live in the moment?

29. "Yesterday is history. Tomorrow is a mystery. Today is a gift. That's why we call it The Present."

(Eleanor Roosevelt (1884-1962)- Political Activist & First Lady of the United States, wife of President Franklin D. Roosevelt (1933-1945))

How do you view your past, present, and future? Do you dwell on your history and consider how you could have changed it? Do you live in the present every day like it could be your last? Or do you focus on the future and what is ahead of you? Is there one way of thinking that is better than another? Or is it better to live in all three?

Inspirational Quotes

30. "We grow great by dreams."

(Woodrow Wilson (1856-1924)- 28th President of the United States (1913-1921))

Why is it important to have goals for your future? What would our world look like if no one ever followed their dreams? Is it essential to support others in their dreams?

31. "There are no secrets to success. It is the result of preparation, hard work, and learning from failure."

(Colin Powell (1937-2021)- 65th United States Secretary of State (2001-2005) & Politician)

Who is the most successful person you know? Why are they successful? How did they get to where they are, and was it easy or hard? Would they follow the same path, or would they get there differently? Do you look up to this person?

32. "If you can't feed a hundred people, then just feed one."

(Margaret Mead (1901-1978)- American cultural anthropologist (She studied the people of the Pacific Islands)

What kind of difference can you make in one person's life? What type of action would you take to help them? What if you couldn't help them? Then what steps would you take?

Inspirational Quotes

33. "No act of kindness, no matter how small, is ever wasted."

(Aesop (620 BCE-564 BCE)- Greek Author & Storyteller "Aesop Fables")

Have you ever made a difference, good or bad, in someone's life and not even realized it until maybe months or years later? How did you find out what you did? What did you do, and what feelings did it give you? Do you regret what you did?

34. "Go confidently in the direction of your dreams. Live the life you On have imagined."

(Henry David Thoreau (1817-1862)- American Philosopher & Author and Poet "Walden" (1854))

What if no one supported you in what you wanted to do and tried to stop you? What would you do? Would you try to explain and reason with these people about your decisions? Or would you go ahead no matter what anyone said or tried to do?

35. "Always keep a positive mindset. It will improve your outlook on the world."

(Roald Dahl (1916-1990)- British Author "Charlie and the Chocolate Factory" (1964))

How do you look at life? Are you a "glass is half full" or a "glass is half empty" kind of person? What are the benefits and drawbacks of each of these frames of mind? Is one better than the other?

Where learning language online is fun!

Inspirational Quotes

36. "No one can make you feel inferior without your consent."

(Eleanor Roosevelt- Political Activist & First Lady of the United States from 1933 to 1945, wife of President Franklin D. Roosevelt)

How do you deal with someone who makes you feel inferior? Do you confront that person and tell them you will not tolerate this treatment? Or do you endure their treatment and never engage them?

37. "The secret of getting ahead is getting started."

(Mark Twain (1835-1910)- American Author "The Adventures of Tom Sawyer (1876))

Are you willing to work hard now and complete any tasks so you can relax and enjoy yourself later? Or do you relax, finish your responsibilities, and hope you finish in time? What are the pros and cons of working these ways?

38. "That which does not kill us makes us stronger."

(Friedrich Nietzsche (1844-1900)- German Philosopher)

Talk about a time when something devastating happened, and you were able to persevere. What steps did you take to overcome the event? How did this event change you? Did you learn anything from what happened?

Where learning language online is fun!

Don't forget to check out our other books, Daily Vocabulary Worksheets Volume 1 and 2 & Daily Vocabulary Flashcards Volume 1 and 2.

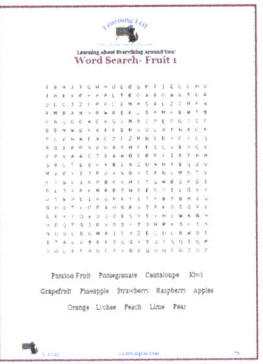

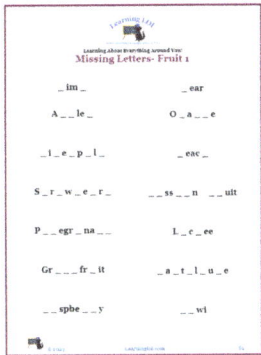

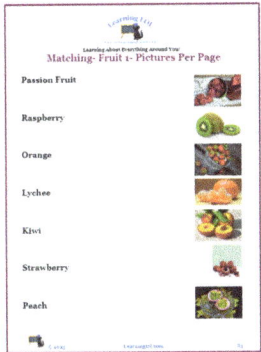

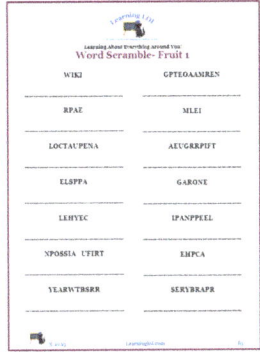

Where learning language online is fun!

www.ingramcontent.com/pod-product-compliance
Lightning Source LLC
Chambersburg PA
CBHW041521120626

46551CB00018B/2520